BACH
FOR BANJO

ARRANGED BY MARK PHILLIPS, JON PEIK AND JIM SCHUSTEDT

T0131124

CONTENTS

ISBN 978-1-61780-375-8

HAL•LEONARD® CORPORATION
7777 W. BLUEMOUND RD. P.O. BOX 13819 MILWAUKEE, WI 53213

In Australia Contact:
Hal Leonard Australia Pty. Ltd.
4 Lentara Court
Cheltenham, Victoria, 3192 Australia
Email: ausadmin@halleonard.com.au

Visit Hal Leonard Online at
www.halleonard.com

Air on the G String

By Johann Sebastian Bach

G tuning:
(5th-1st) G-D-G-B-D

Key of C

Slowly

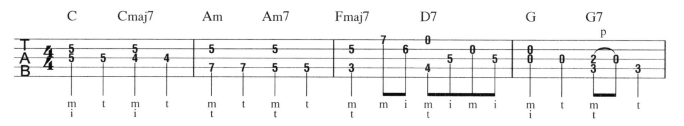

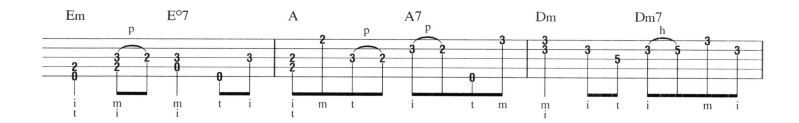

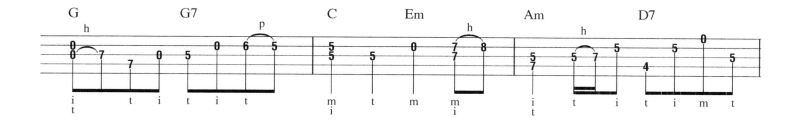

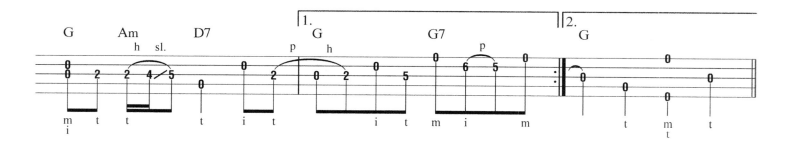

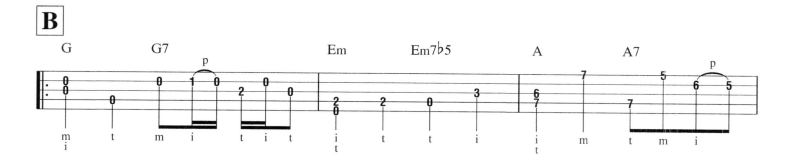

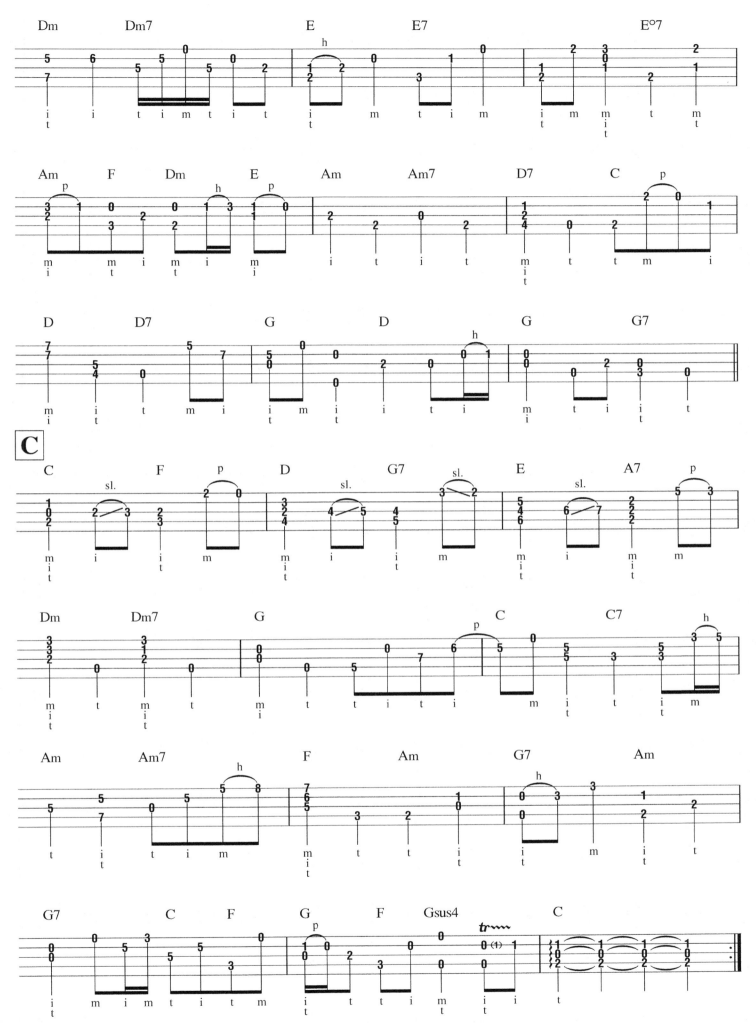

Arioso

By Johann Sebastian Bach

G tuning:
(5th-1st) G-D-G-B-D

Key of G

Slowly

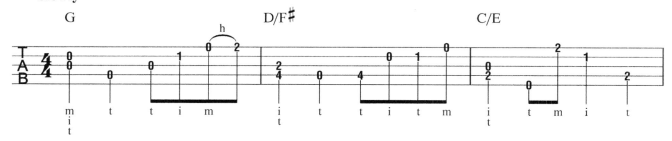

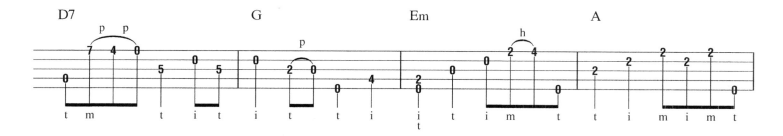

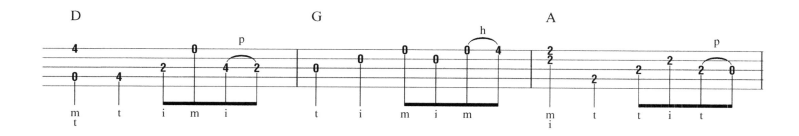

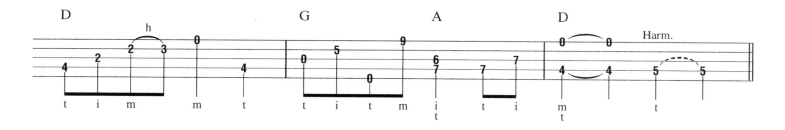

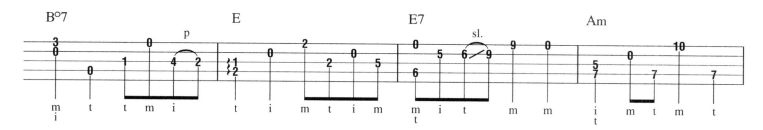

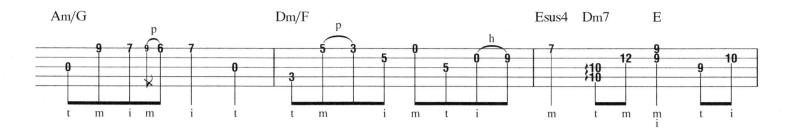

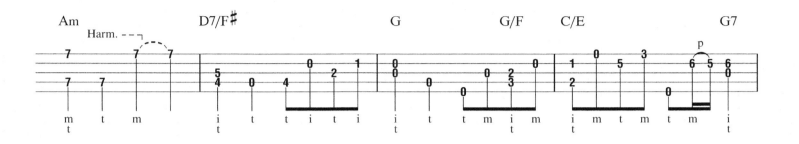

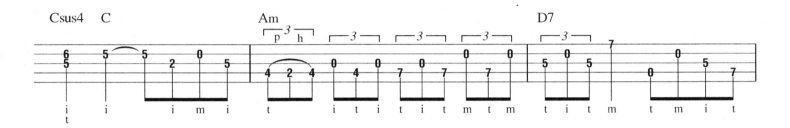

C

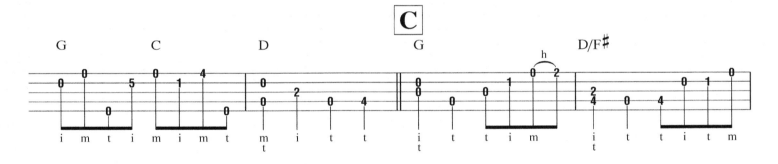

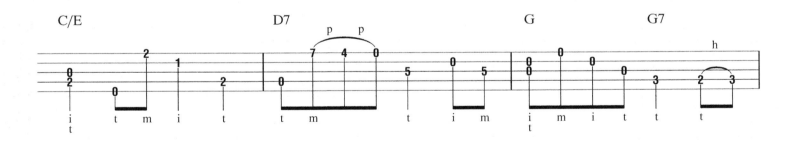

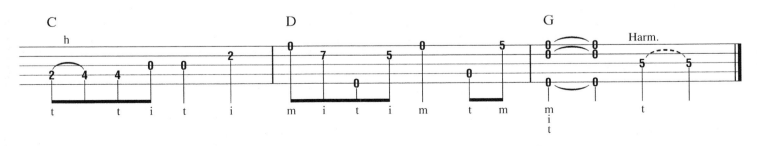

Be Thou with Me
(from the *Anna Magdalena Notebook*)

By Johann Sebastian Bach

G tuning:
(5th-1st) G-D-G-B-D

Key of G

Moderately

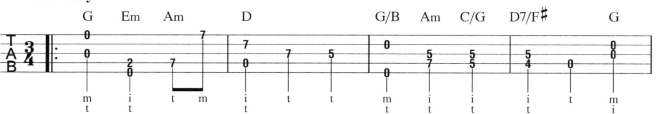

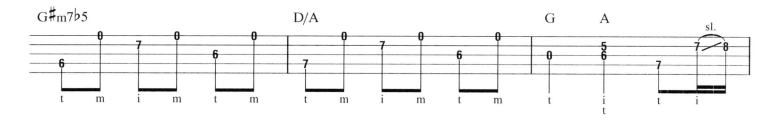

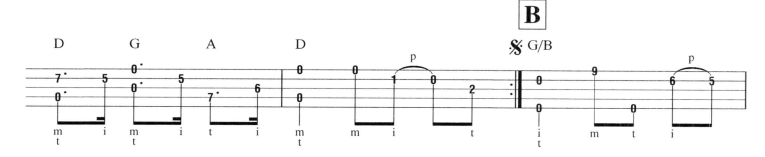

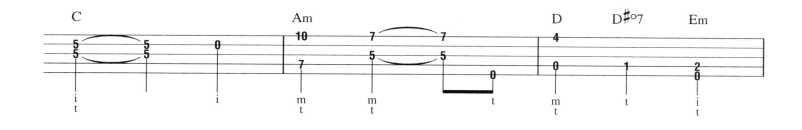

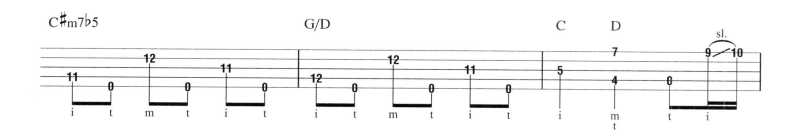

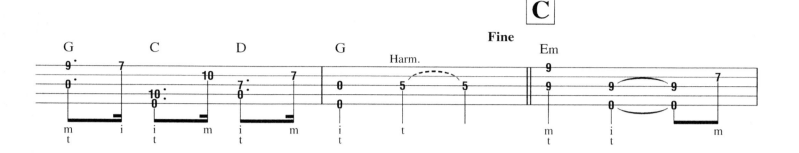

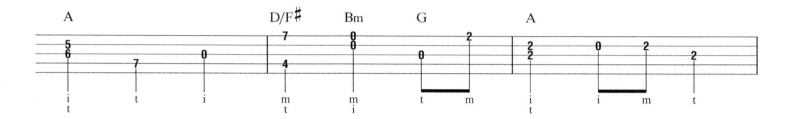

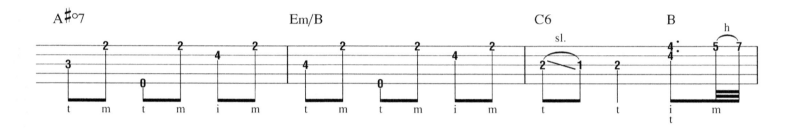

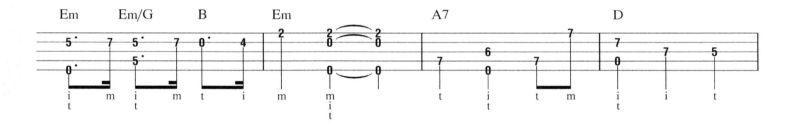

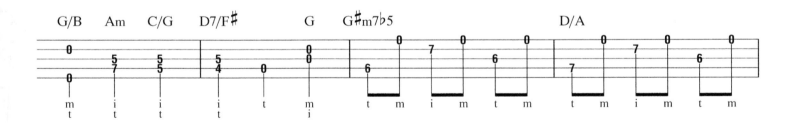

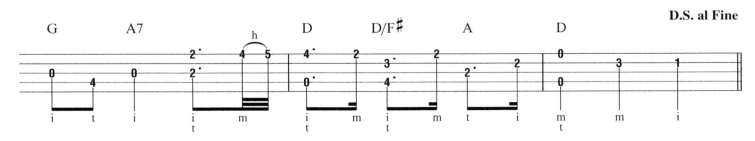

Bourrée
(from Cello Suite No. 3)

By Johann Sebastian Bach

G tuning:
(5th-1st) G-D-G-B-D

Key of G

Moderately

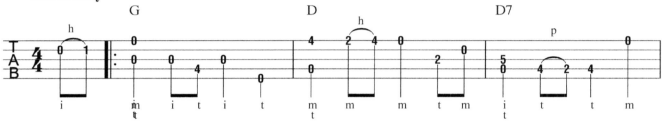

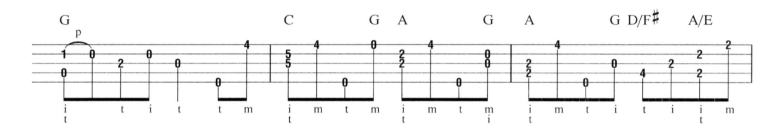

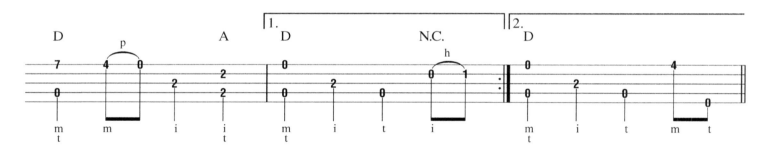

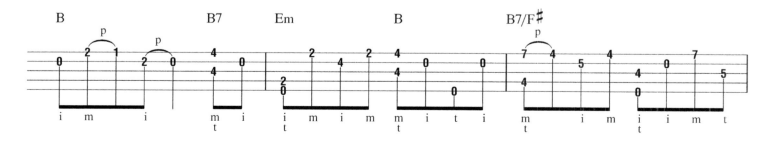

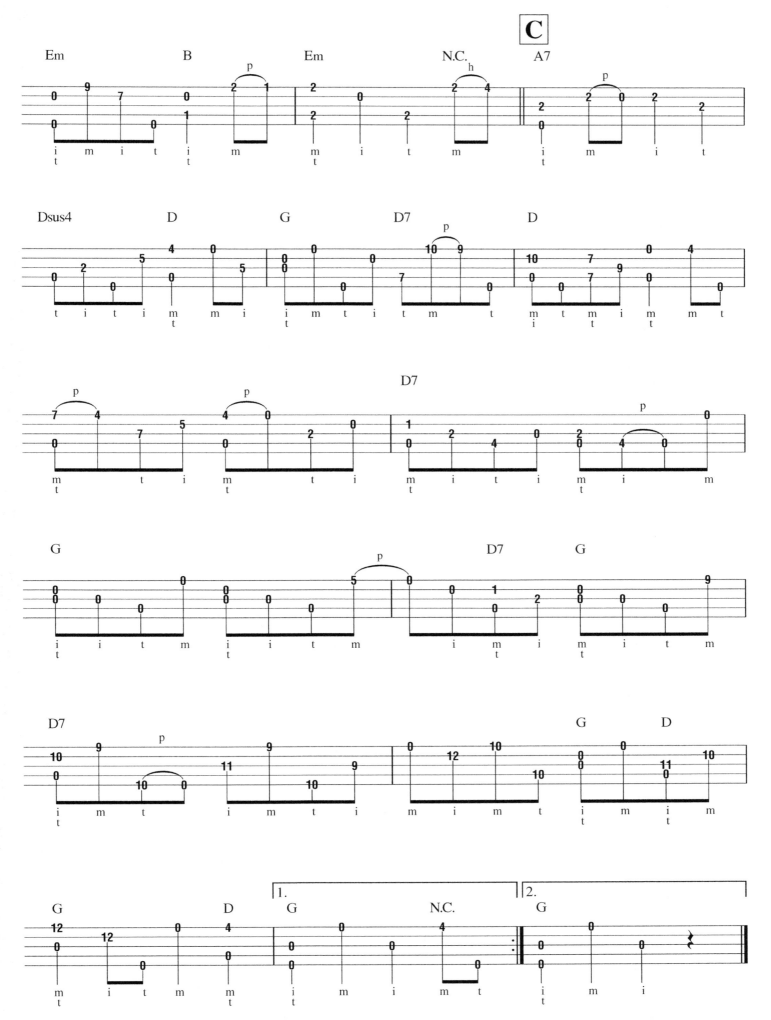

Bourrée in E Minor

By Johann Sebastian Bach

G tuning:
(5th-1st) G-D-G-B-D

Key of E minor

Moderately

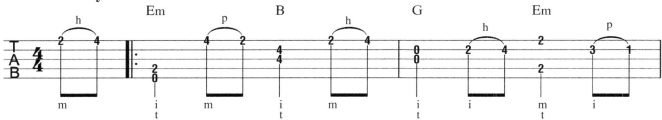

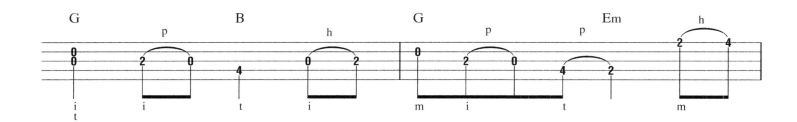

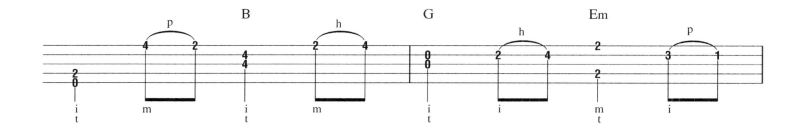

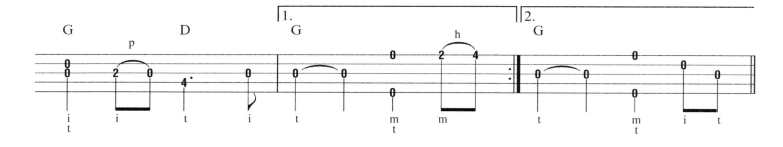

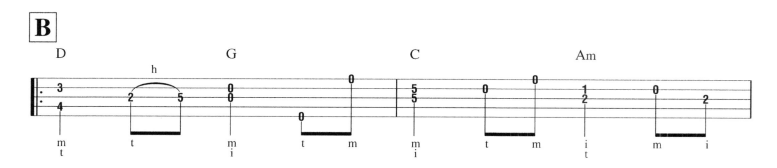

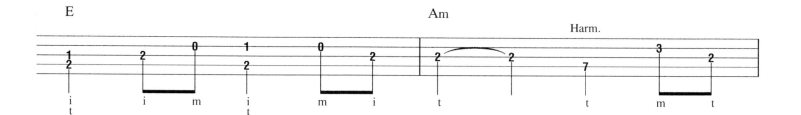

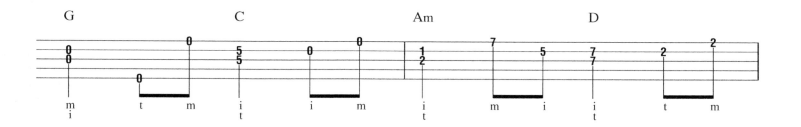

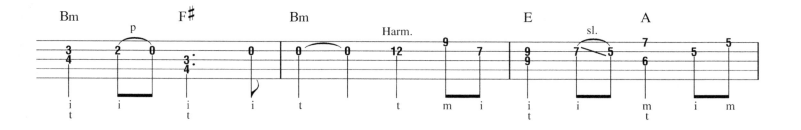

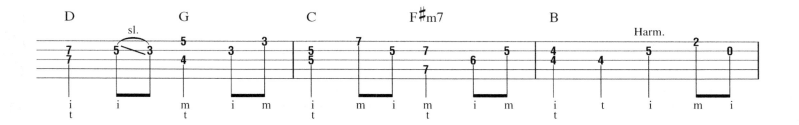

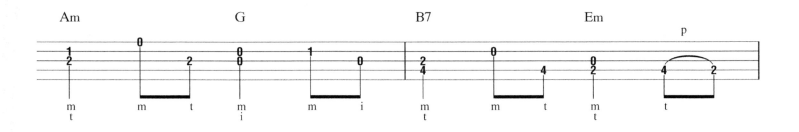

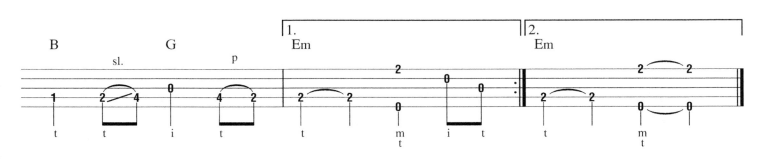

Brandenburg Concerto No. 3
First Movement
By Johann Sebastian Bach

Tuning:
(5th-1st) G-D-G-B-D

Key of G

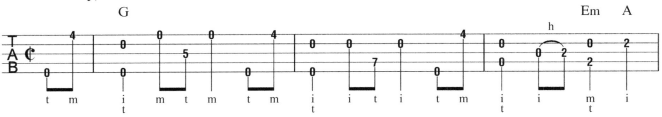

Moderately, in 2

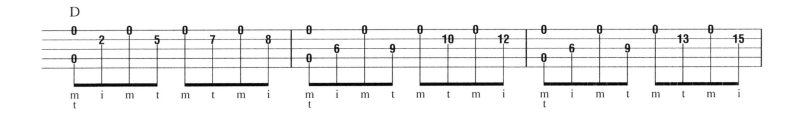

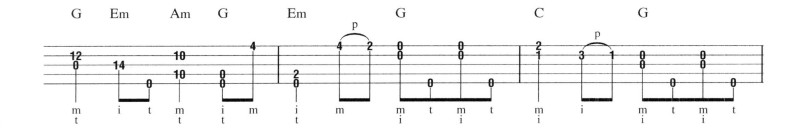

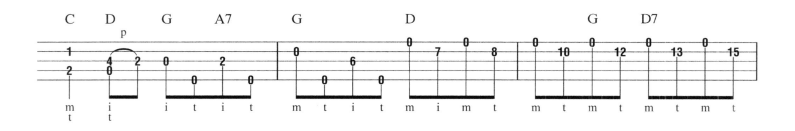

To Coda ⊕

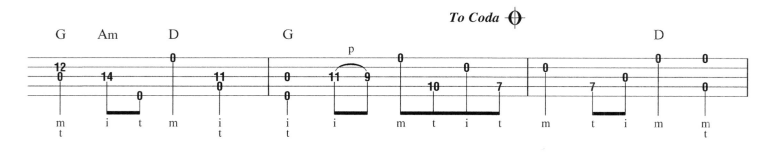

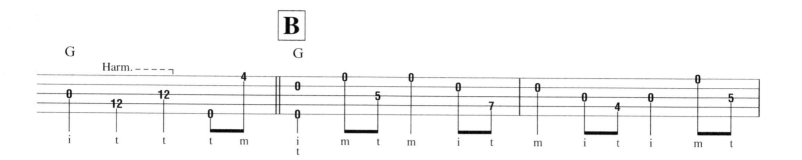

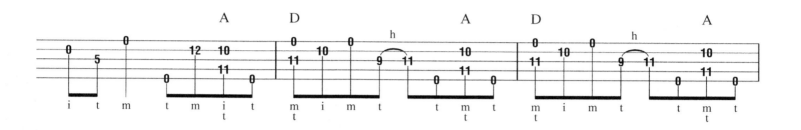

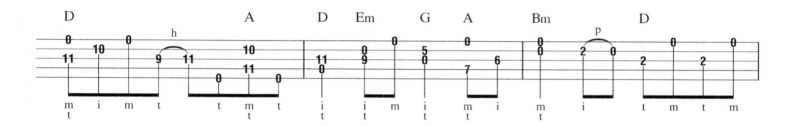

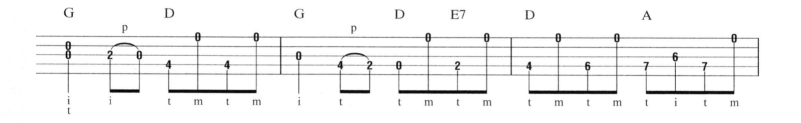

D.S. al Coda

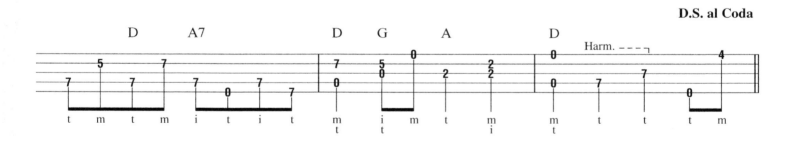

⊕ Coda

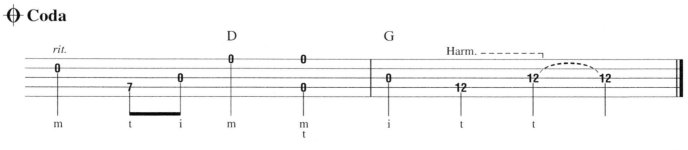

Gavotte
(from French Suite No. 5)

By Johann Sebastian Bach

G tuning:
(5th-1st) G-D-G-B-D

Key of G

Moderately, in 2

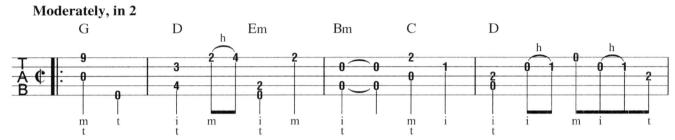

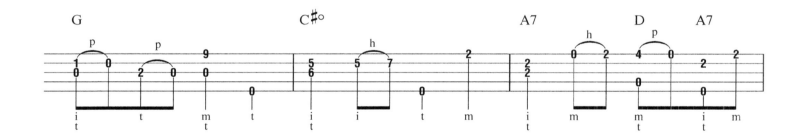

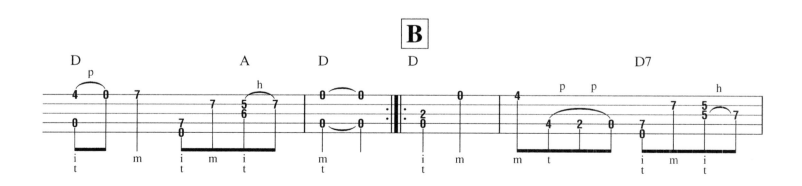

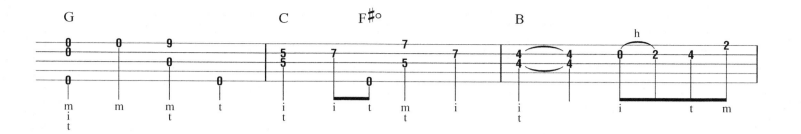

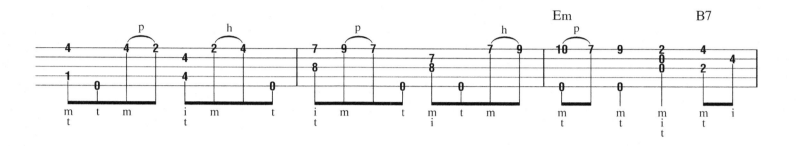

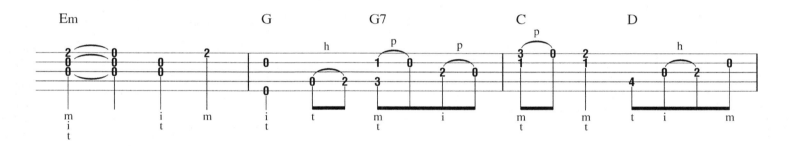

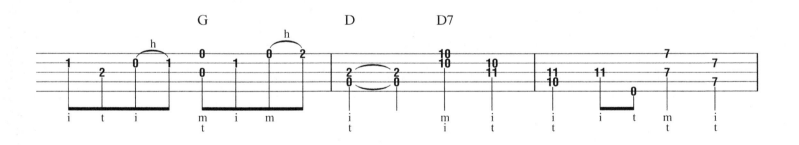

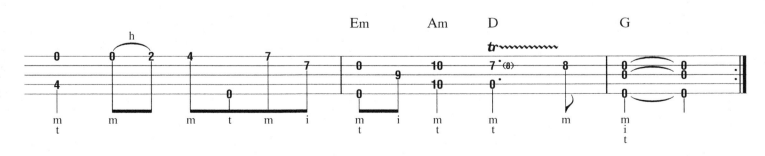

Gavotte
(from Cello Suite No. 6)

By Johann Sebastian Bach

G tuning:
(5th-1st) G-D-G-B-D

Key of D

Moderately, in 2

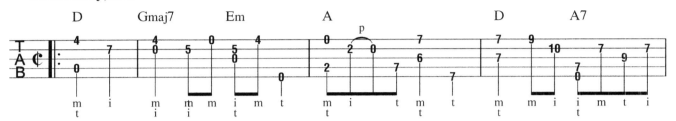

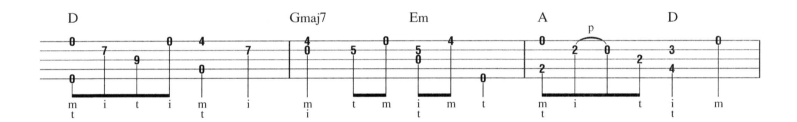

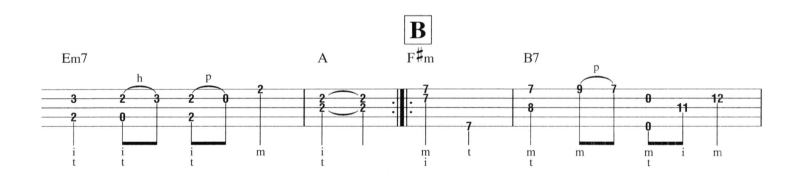

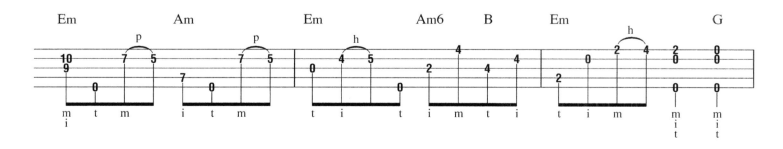

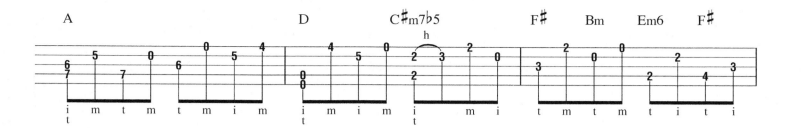

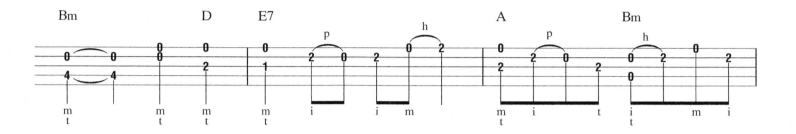

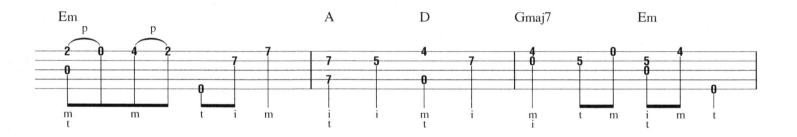

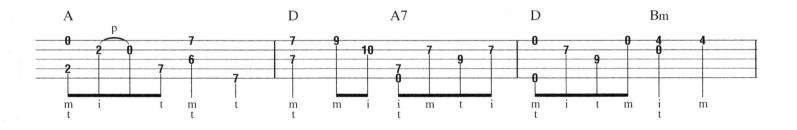

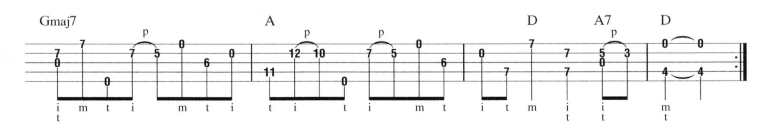

Chorale
(from *St. Matthew Passion*)

By Johann Sebastian Bach

G tuning:
(5th-1st) G-D-G-B-D

Key of C

Moderately

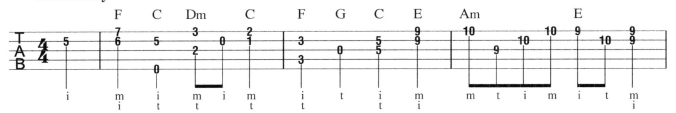

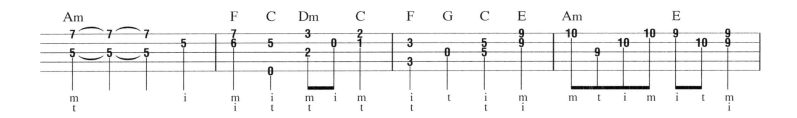

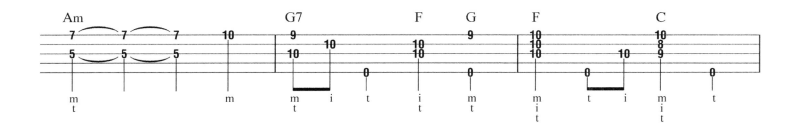

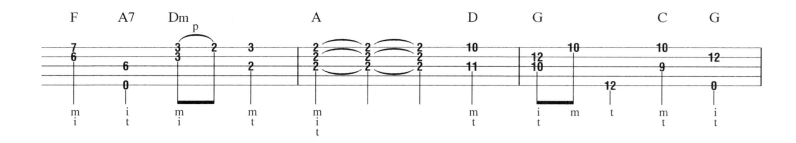

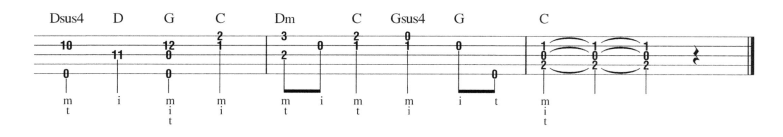

Jesu, Joy of Man's Desiring
(from Cantata No. 147)

By Johann Sebastian Bach

G tuning:
(5th-1st) G-D-G-B-D

Key of G

Moderately slow

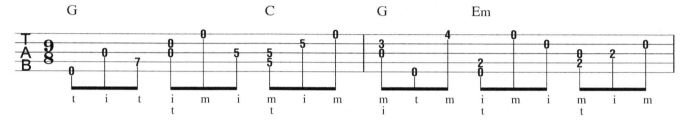

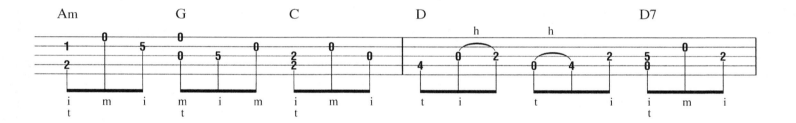

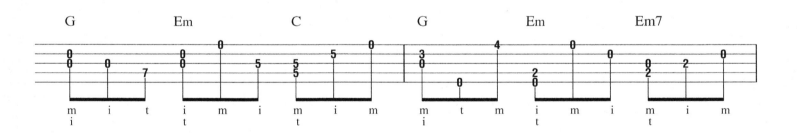

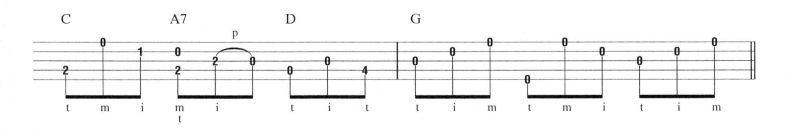

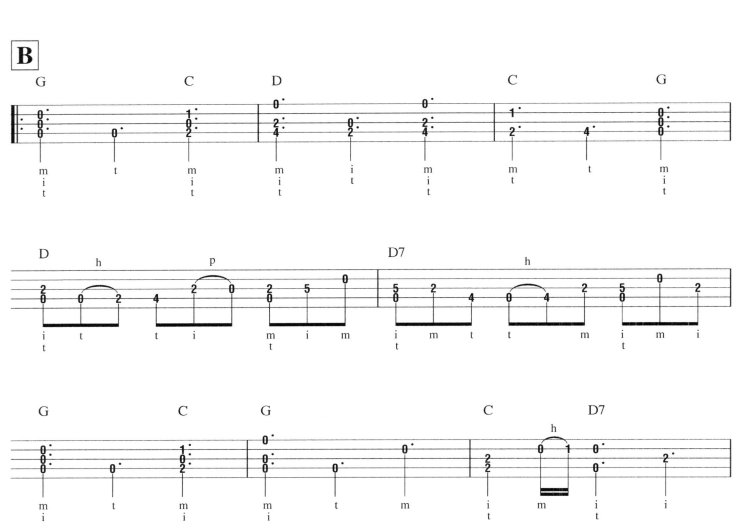

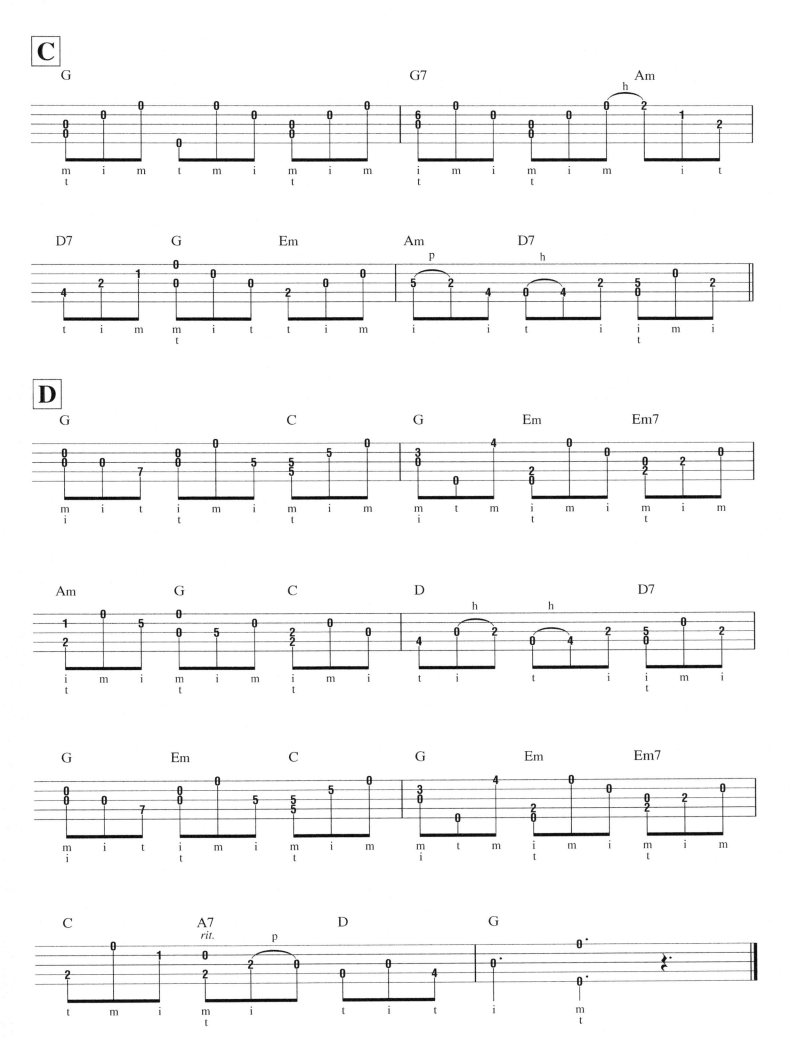

Keep, O My Spirit

By Johann Sebastian Bach

G tuning:
(5th-1st) G-D-G-B-D

Key of E minor

Moderately slow

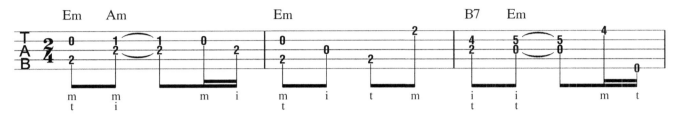

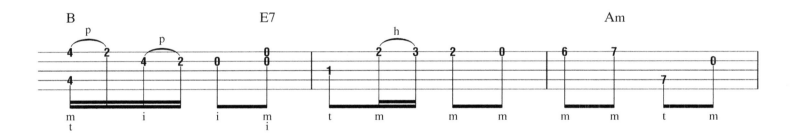

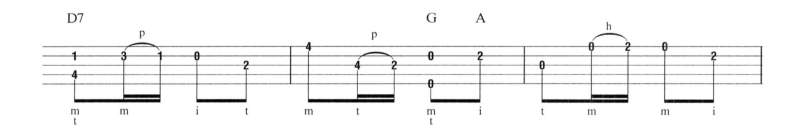

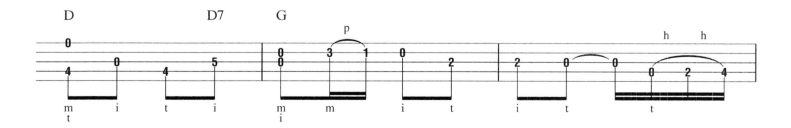

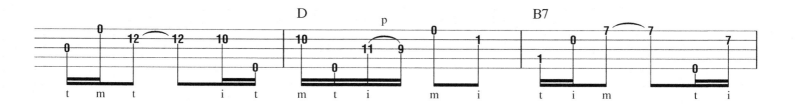

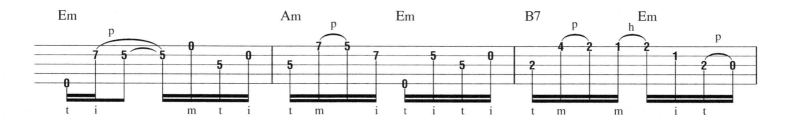

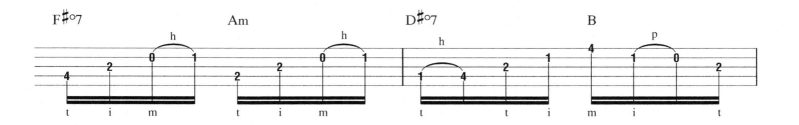

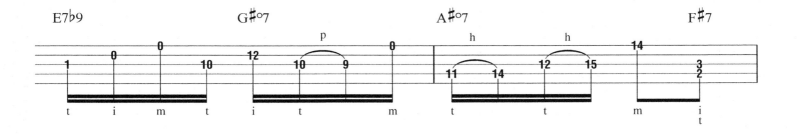

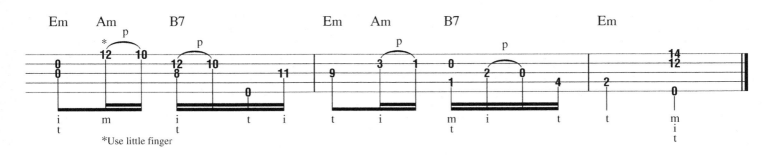

*Use little finger

Little Prelude No. 2

By Johann Sebastian Bach

G tuning:
(5th-1st) G-D-G-B-D

Key of G

Moderately

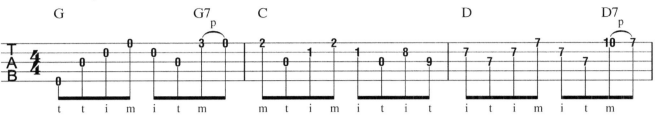

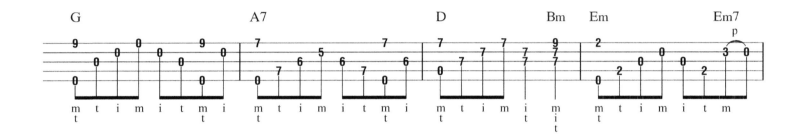

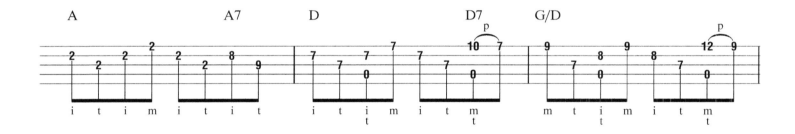

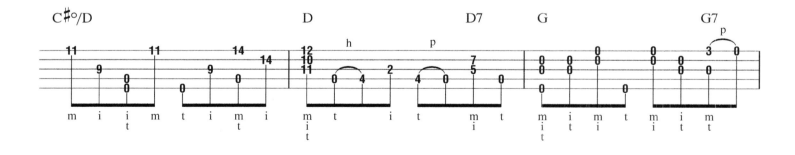

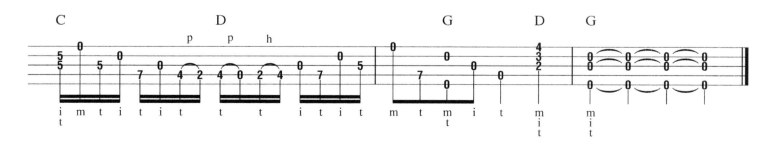

Minuet in G

By Johann Sebastian Bach

G tuning:
(5th-1st) G-D-G-B-D

Key of G

Moderately

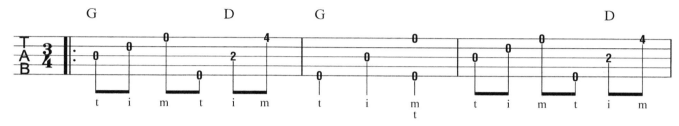

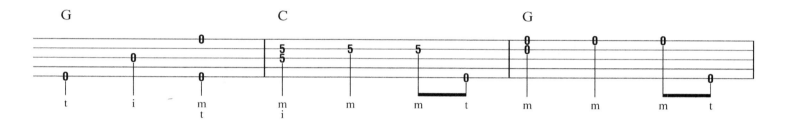

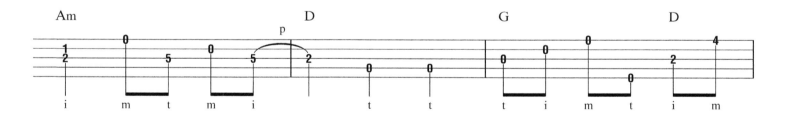

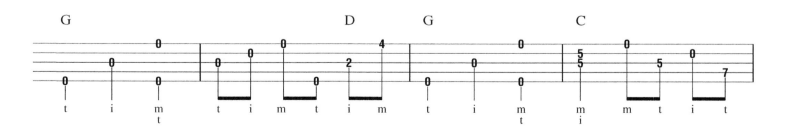

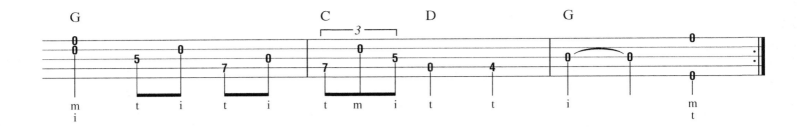

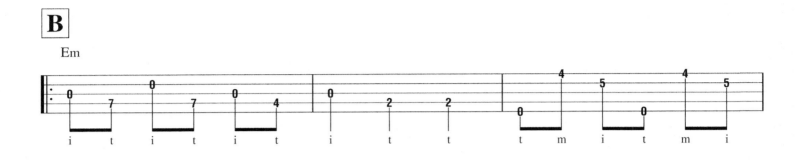

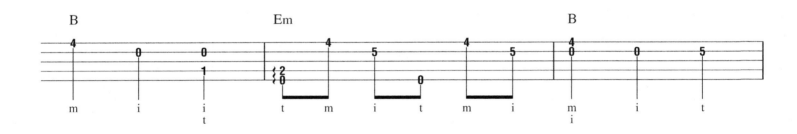

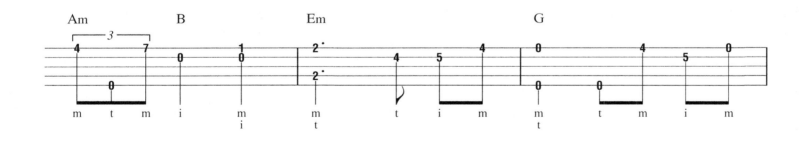

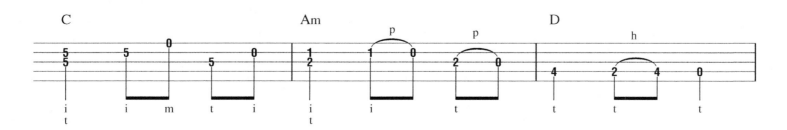

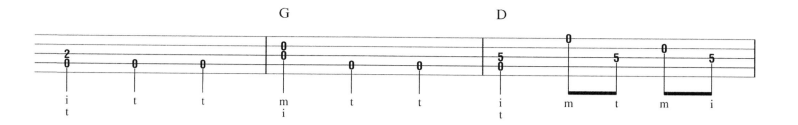

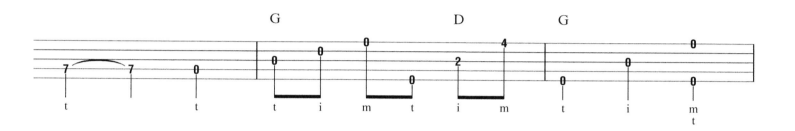

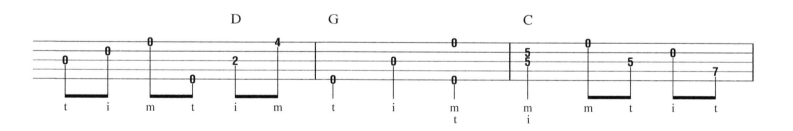

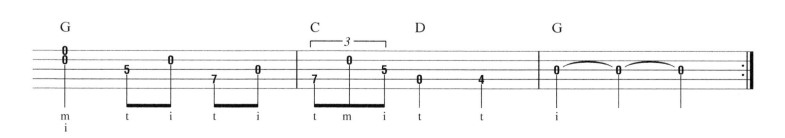

Minuet I
(from the *Anna Magdalena Notebook*)

By Johann Sebastian Bach

G tuning:
(5th-1st) G-D-G-B-D

Key of G

Moderately

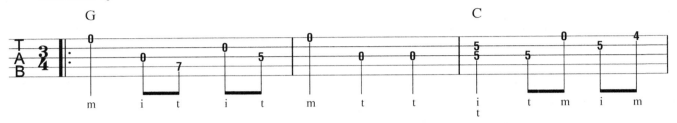

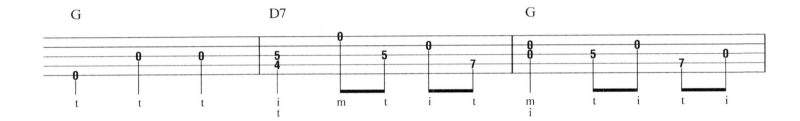

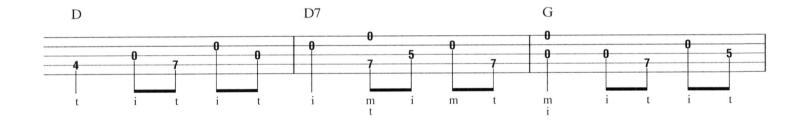

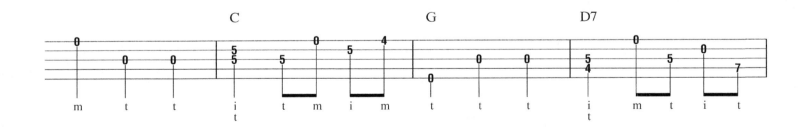

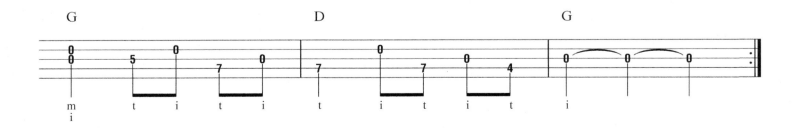

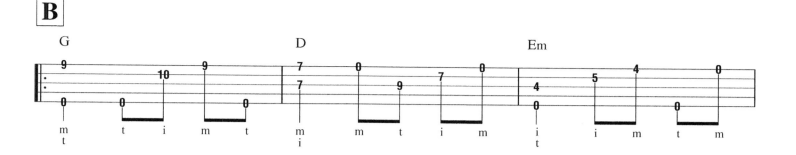

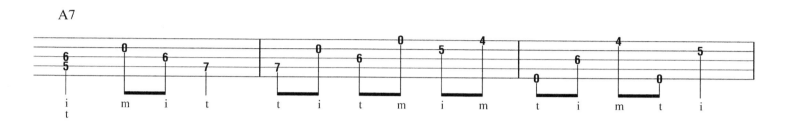

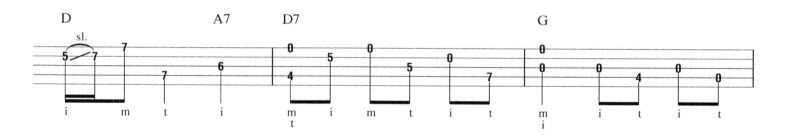

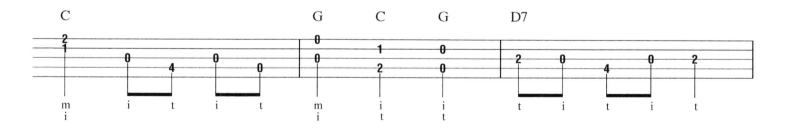

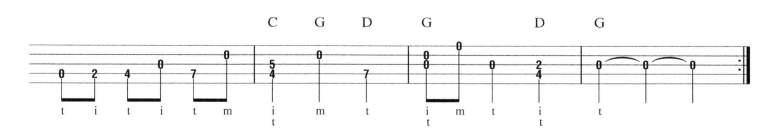

Prelude
(from Cello Suite No. 1)

By Johann Sebastian Bach

C tuning:
(5th-1st) G-C-G-B-D

Key of C

Moderately slow

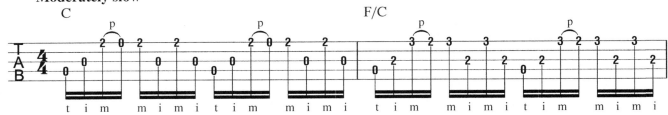

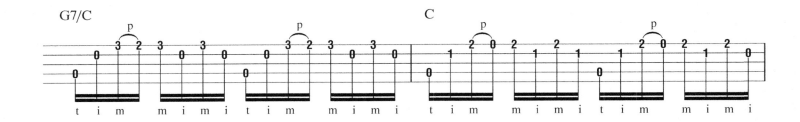

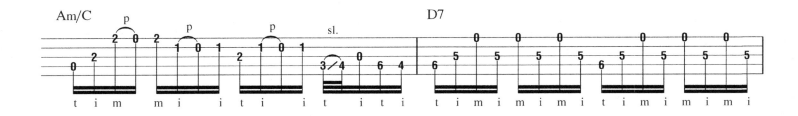

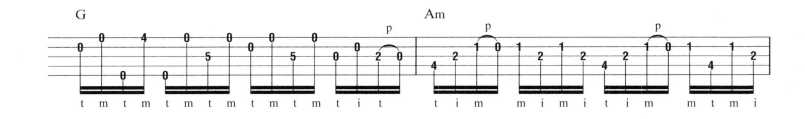

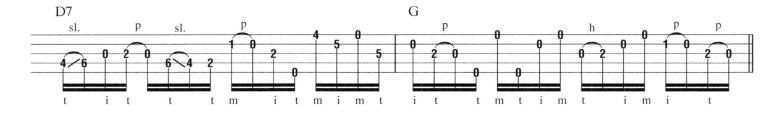

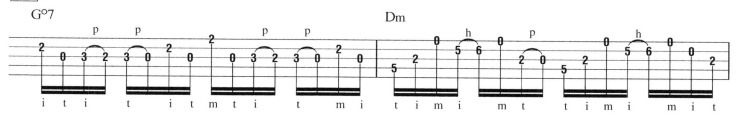

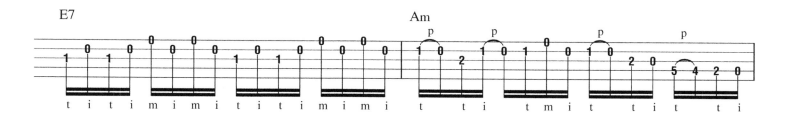

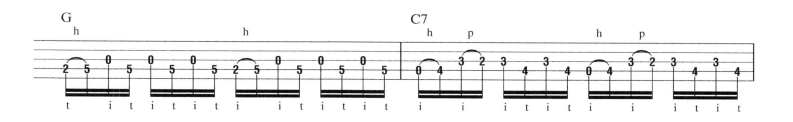

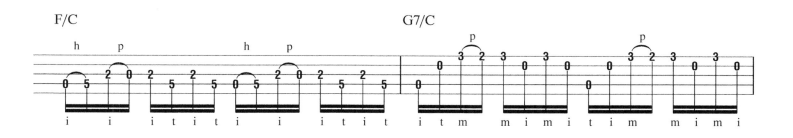

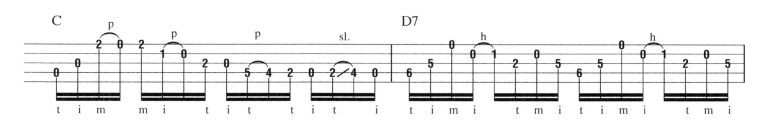

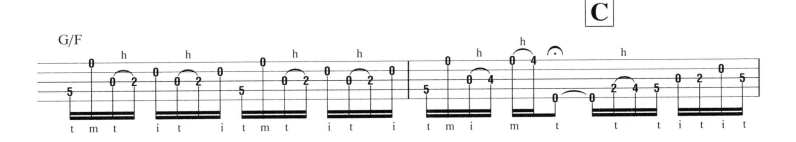

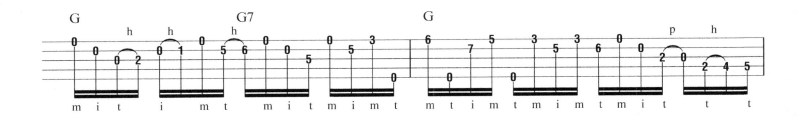

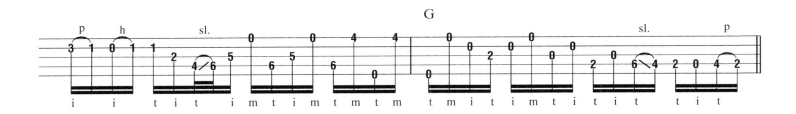

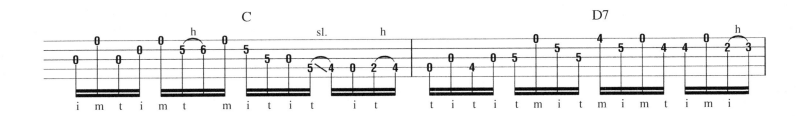

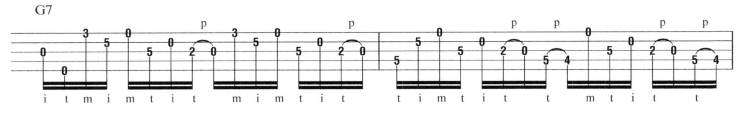

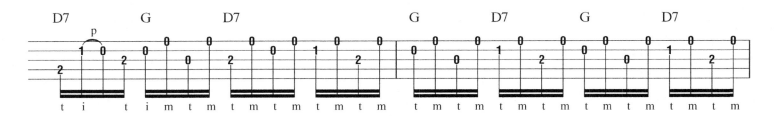

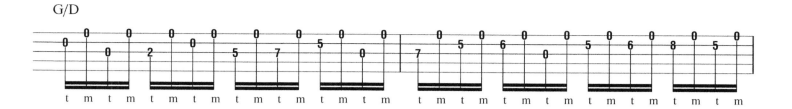

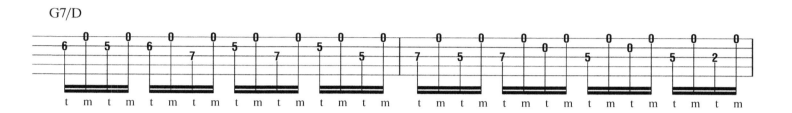

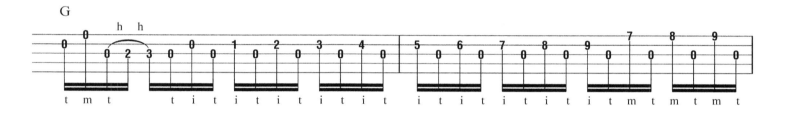

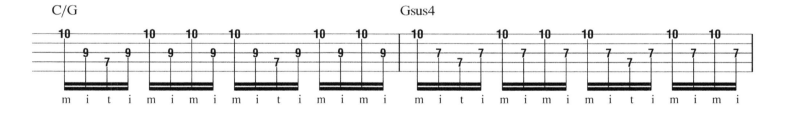

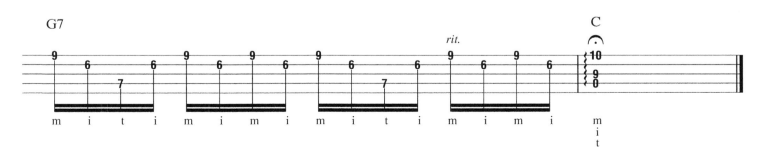

Prelude
(from Violin Partita No. 3)
By Johann Sebastian Bach

G tuning:
(5th-1st) G-D-G-B-D

Key of G

Moderately

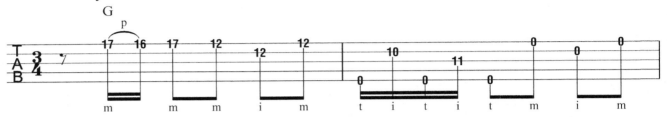

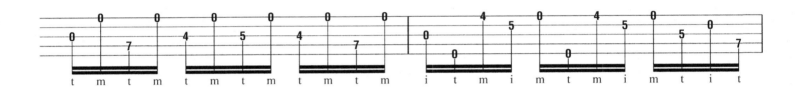

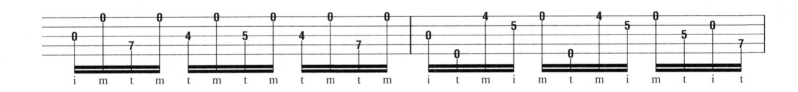

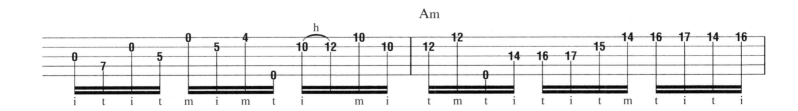

G

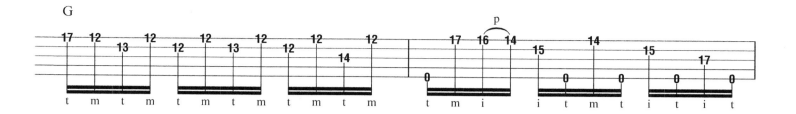

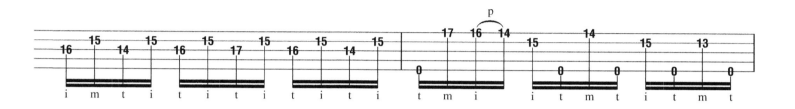

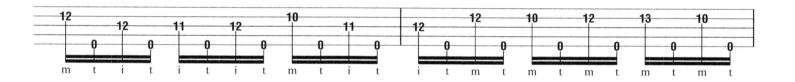

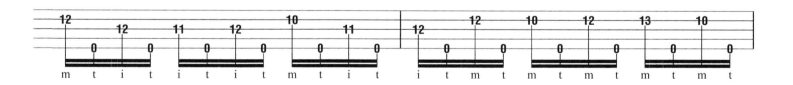

Gmaj7

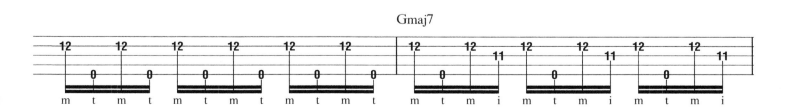

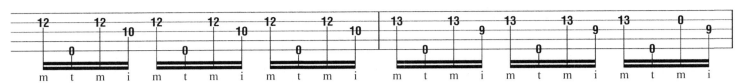

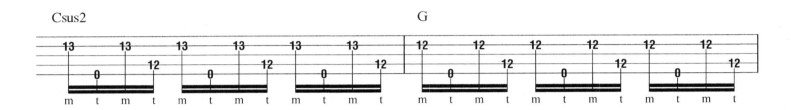

Csus2   G

Cmaj7   C6

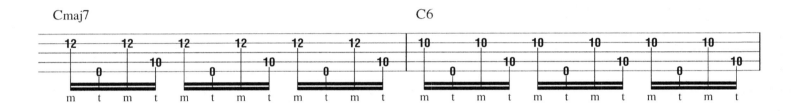

Gsus2/B   G

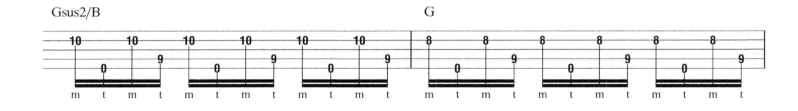

D   G   D   G

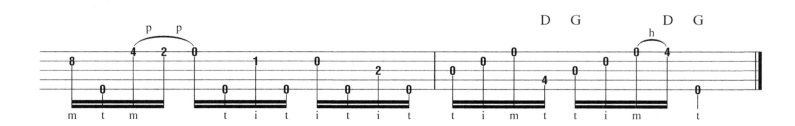

Prelude in C Major

(from *The Well-Tempered Clavier, Book I*)

By Johann Sebastian Bach

G tuning:
(5th-1st) G-D-G-B-D

Key of C

Moderately

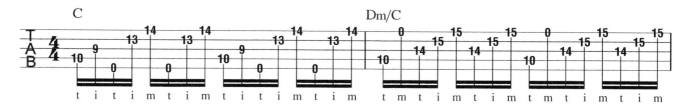

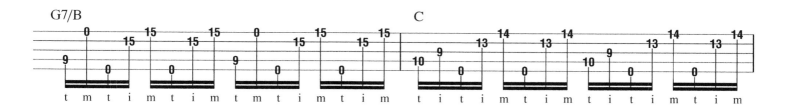

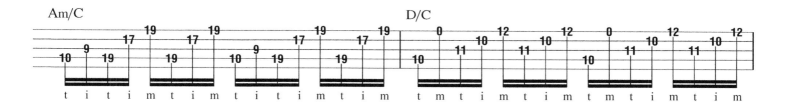

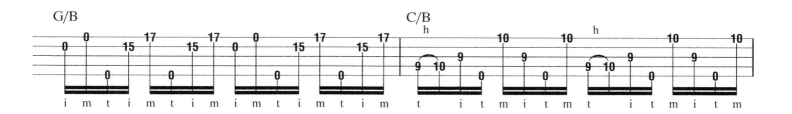

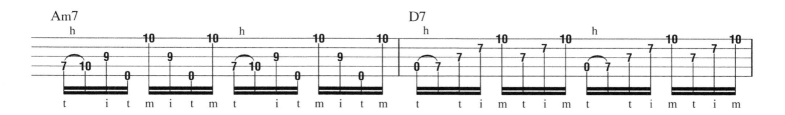

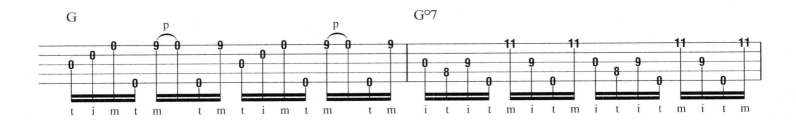

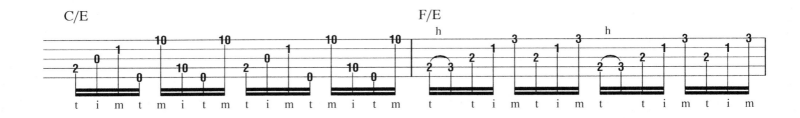

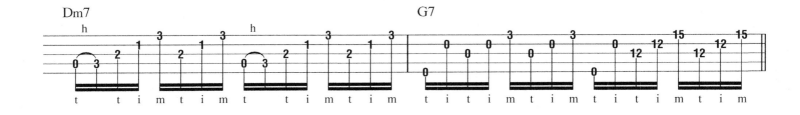

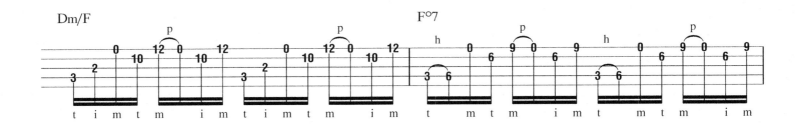

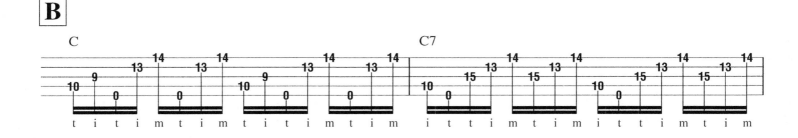

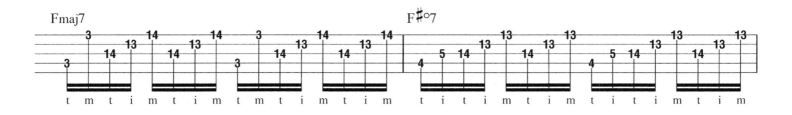

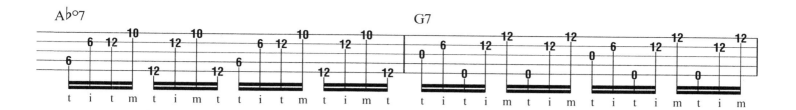

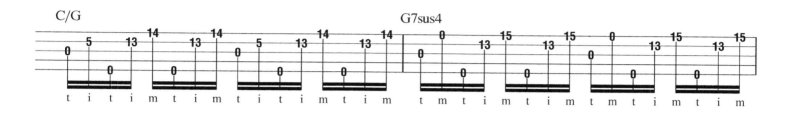

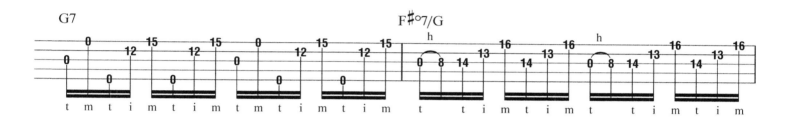

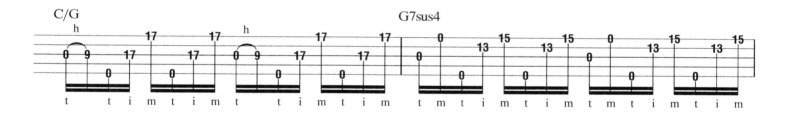

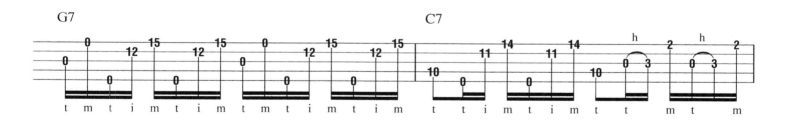

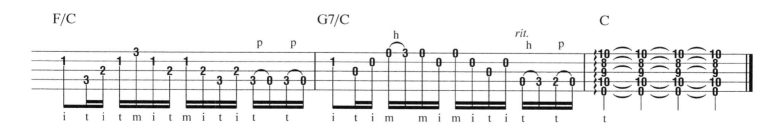

Sheep May Safely Graze

(from Cantata No. 208)

By Johann Sebastian Bach

Tuning:
(5th-1st) F♯-D-G-B-D

Key of D

A

Moderately slow, in 2

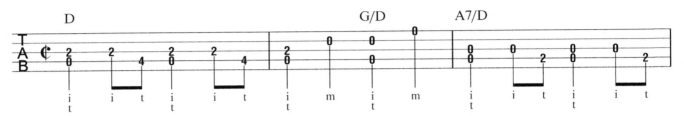

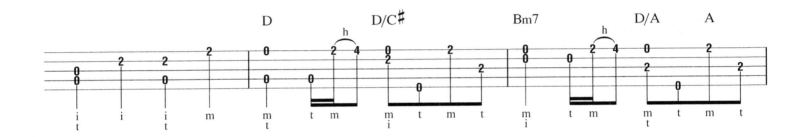

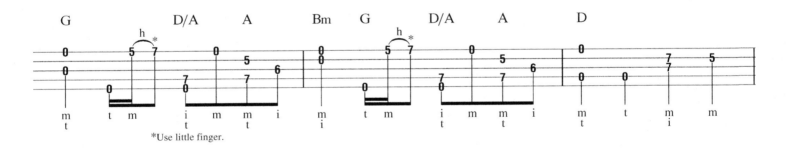

*Use little finger.

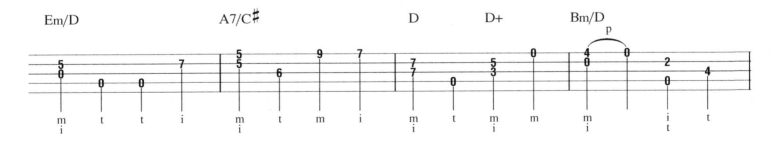

B

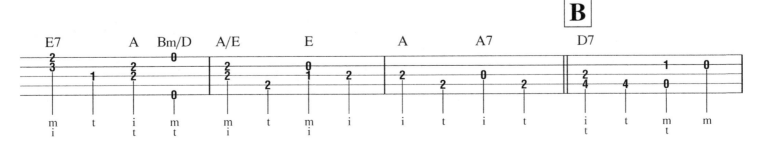

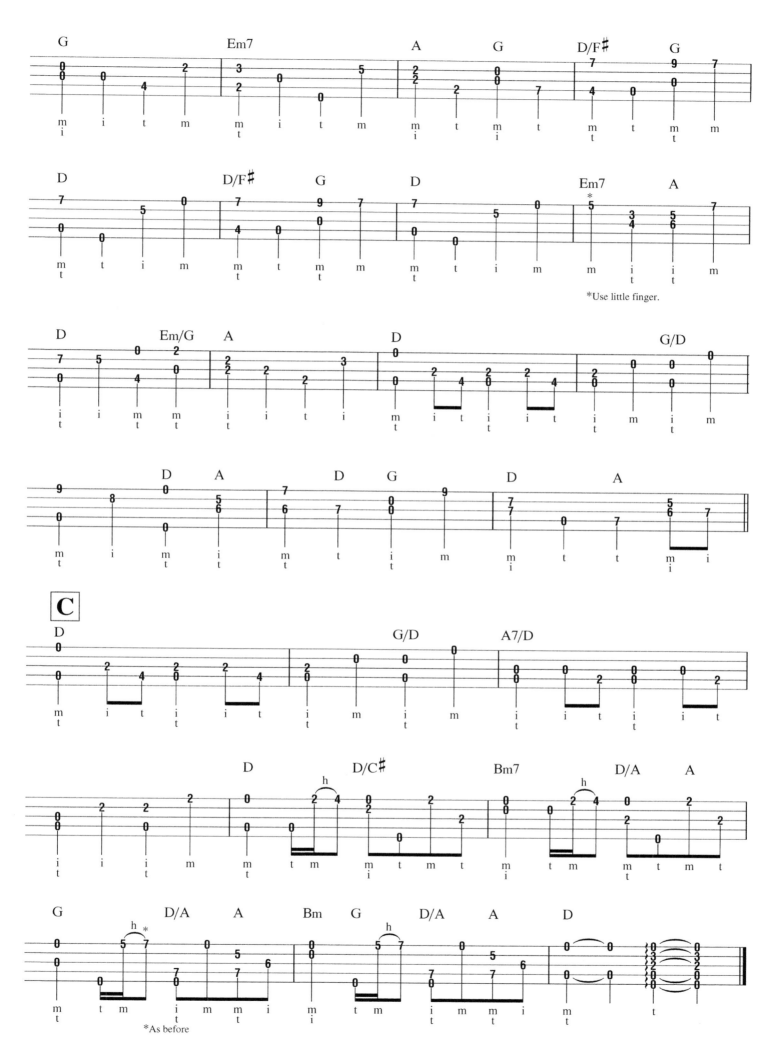

*Use little finger.

*As before

41

Siciliano
(from Flute Sonata No. 2)

By Johann Sebastian Bach

G minor tuning:
(5th–1st) G-D-G-B♭-D

Key of G minor

Slowly, in 2

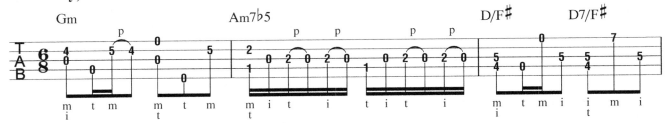

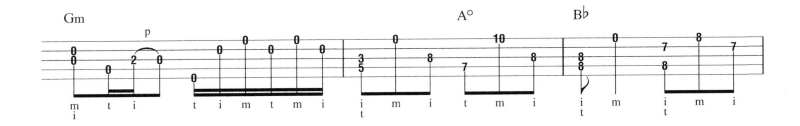

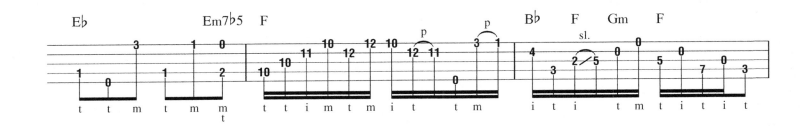

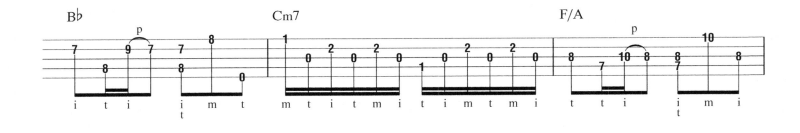

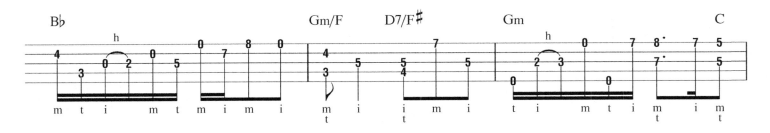

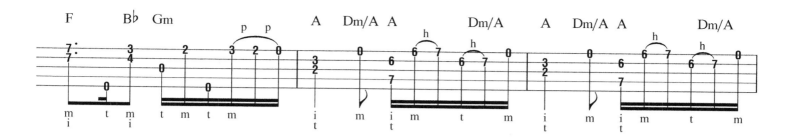

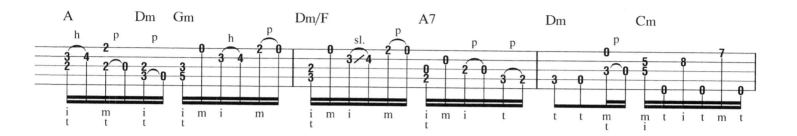

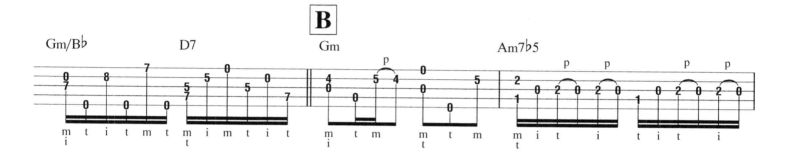

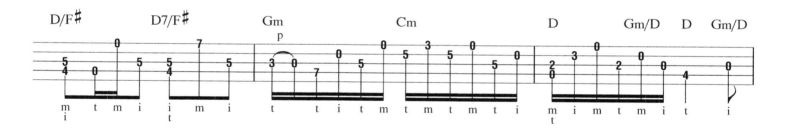

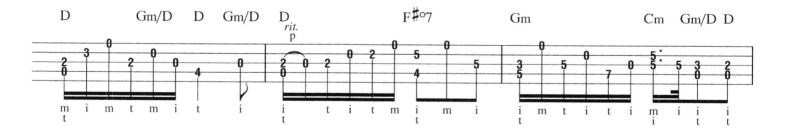

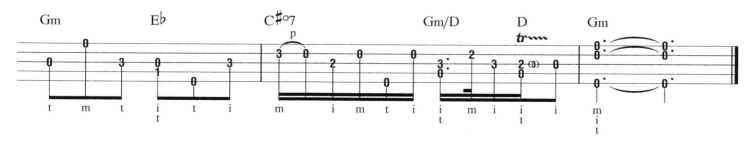

Sleepers, Awake
(from Cantata No. 140)

By Johann Sebastian Bach

Tuning:
(5th-1st) F#-D-G-B-D

Key of D

Moderately slow

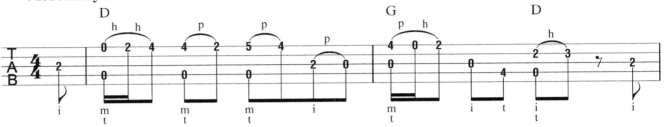

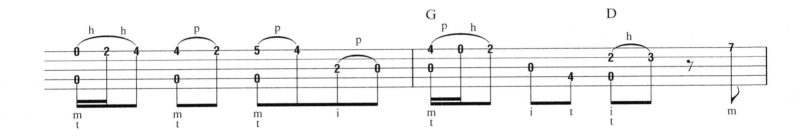

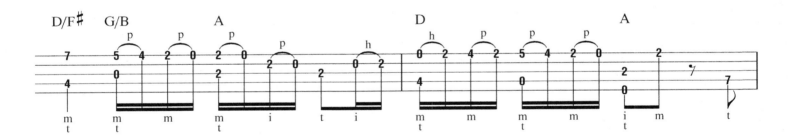

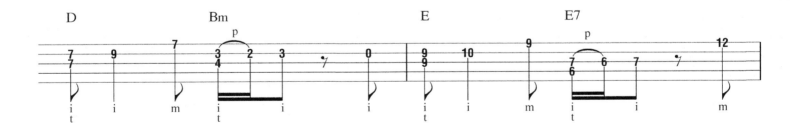

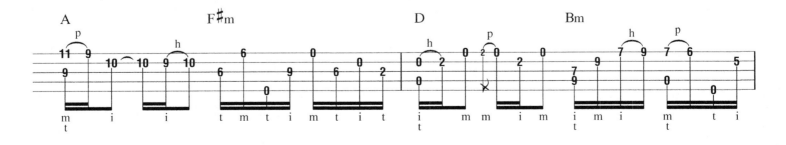

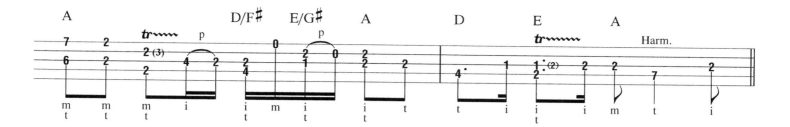

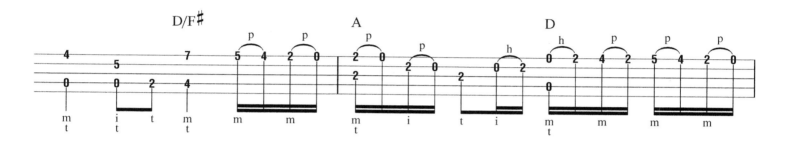

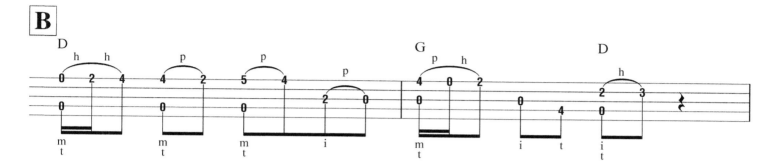

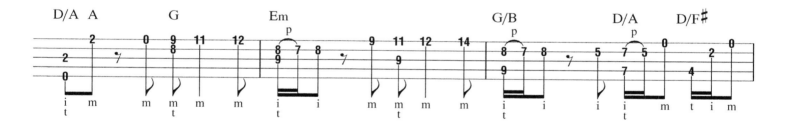

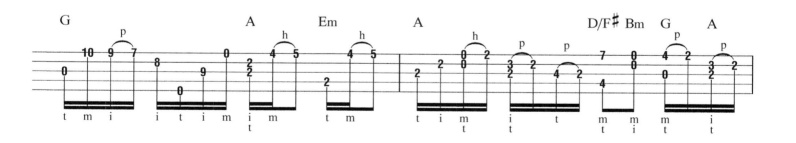

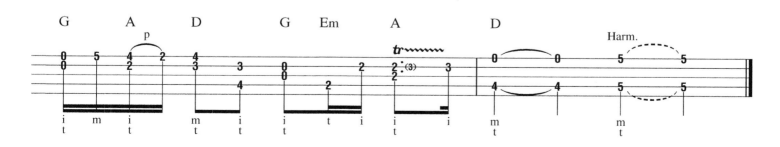

GREAT BANJO PUBLICATIONS

FROM HAL LEONARD

Hal Leonard Banjo Method

by Mac Robertson, Robbie Clement, Will Schmid

This innovative method teaches 5-string banjo bluegrass style using a carefully paced approach that keeps beginners playing great songs *while learning*. Book 1 covers easy chord strums, tablature, right-hand rolls, hammer-ons, slides and pull-offs, and more. Book 2 includes solos and licks, fiddle tunes, back-up, capo use, and more.

00699500 Book 1 Book Only $9.99
00695101 Book 1 Book/Online Audio $17.99
00699502 Book 2 Book Only $9.99

Banjo Chord Finder
00695741 9 x 12...$8.99
00695742 6 x 9...$7.99

Banjo Scale Finder
00695783 6 x 9...$6.99

Banjo Aerobics
A 50-Week Workout Program for Developing, Improving and Maintaining Banjo Technique

by Michael Bremer

Take your banjo playing to the next level with this fantastic daily resource, providing a year's worth of practice material with a two-week vacation. The accompanying audio includes demo tracks for all the examples in the book to reinforce how the banjo should sound.

00113734 Book/Online Audio $22.99

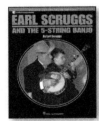

Earl Scruggs and the 5-String Banjo

Earl Scruggs' legendary method has helped thousands of banjo players get their start. It features everything you need to know to start playing, even how to build your own banjo! Topics covered include: Scruggs tuners • how to read music • chords • how to read tablature • anatomy of Scruggs-style picking • exercises in picking • 44 songs • biographical notes • and more! The online audio features Earl Scruggs playing and explaining over 60 examples!

00695764 Book Only..$29.99
00695765 Book/Online Audio $39.99

First 50 Songs You Should Play on Banjo

arr. Michael J. Miles & Greg Cahill

Easy-to-read banjo tab, chord symbols and lyrics for the most popular songs banjo players like to play. Explore clawhammer and three-finger-style banjo in a variety of tunings and capoings with this one-of-a-kind collection. Songs include: Angel from Montgomery • Carolina in My Mind • Cripple Creek • Danny Boy • The House of the Rising Sun • Mr. Tambourine Man • Take Me Home, Country Roads • This Land Is Your Land • Wildwood Flower • and many more.

00153311 ....$15.99

Fretboard Roadmaps

by Fred Sokolow

This handy book/with online audio will get you playing all over the banjo fretboard in any key! You'll learn to: increase your chord, scale and lick vocabulary • play chord-based licks, moveable major and blues scales, melodic scales and first-position major scales • and much more! The audio includes 51 demonstrations of the exercises.

00695358 Book/Online Audio $17.99

The Great American Banjo Songbook
70 Songs

arr. Alan Munde & Beth Mead-Sullivan

Explore the repertoire of the "Great American Songbook" with this 70-song collection, masterfully arranged by Alan Munde and Beth Mead-Sullivan for 3-finger, Scruggs-style 5-string banjo. Rhythm tab, right hand fingerings and chord diagrams are included for each of these beloved melodies. Songs include: Ain't She Sweet • Blue Skies • Cheek to Cheek • Home on the Range • Honeysuckle Rose • It Had to Be You • Little Rock Getaway • Over the Rainbow • Sweet Georgia Brown • and more.

00156862 ....$19.99

How to Play the 5-String Banjo
Third Edition

by Pete Seeger

This basic manual for banjo players includes melody line, lyrics and banjo accompaniment and solos notated in standard form and tablature. Chapters cover material such as: a basic strum, the fifth string, hammering on, pulling off, double thumbing, and much more.

14015486 ....$19.99

O Brother, Where Art Thou?

Banjo tab arrangements of 12 bluegrass/folk songs from this Grammy-winning album. Includes: The Big Rock Candy Mountain • Down to the River to Pray • I Am a Man of Constant Sorrow • I Am Weary (Let Me Rest) • I'll Fly Away • In the Jailhouse Now • Keep on the Sunny Side • You Are My Sunshine • and more, plus lyrics and a banjo notation legend.

00699528 Banjo Tablature $17.99

Clawhammer Cookbook
Tools, Techniques & Recipes for Playing Clawhammer Banjo

by Michael Bremer

The goal of this book isn't to tell you how to play tunes or how to play like anyone else. It's to teach you ways to approach, arrange, and personalize any tune – to develop your own unique style. To that end, we'll take in a healthy serving of old-time music and also expand the clawhammer palate to taste a few other musical styles. Includes audio track demos of all the songs and examples to aid in the learning process.

00118354 Book/Online Audio $22.99

The Ultimate Banjo Songbook

A great collection of banjo classics: Alabama Jubilee • Bye Bye Love • Duelin' Banjos • The Entertainer • Foggy Mountain Breakdown • Great Balls of Fire • Lady of Spain • Orange Blossom Special • (Ghost) Riders in the Sky • Rocky Top • San Antonio Rose • Tennessee Waltz • UFO-TOFU • You Are My Sunshine • and more.

00699565 Book/Online Audio $29.99

Visit Hal Leonard online at **www.halleonard.com**

Learn to Play Today
with folk music instruction from Hal Leonard

Hal Leonard Bagpipe Method

The Hal Leonard Bagpipe Method is designed for anyone just learning to play the Great Highland bagpipes. This comprehensive and easy-to-use beginner's guide serves as an introduction to the bagpipe chanter. It includes access to online video lessons with demonstrations of all the examples in the book! Lessons include: the practice chanter, the Great Highland Bagpipe scale, bagpipe notation, proper technique, grace-noting, embellishments, playing and practice tips, traditional tunes, buying a bagpipe, and much more!
00102521 Book/Online Video $14.99

Hal Leonard Banjo Method – Second Edition

Authored by Mac Robertson, Robbie Clement & Will Schmid. This innovative method teaches 5-string, bluegrass style. The method consists of two instruction books and two cross-referenced supplement books that offer the beginner a carefully-paced and interest-keeping approach to the bluegrass style.
00699500 Book 1 Only..........................$9.99
00695101 Book 1 with Online Audio...............$17.99
00699502 Book 2 Only..........................$9.99
00696056 Book 2 with CD..............................$17.99

Hal Leonard Brazilian Guitar Method

by Carlos Arana

This book uses popular Brazilian songs to teach you the basics of the Brazilian guitar style and technique. Learn to play in the styles of Joao Gilberto, Luiz Bonfá, Baden Powell, Dino Sete Cordas, Joao Basco, and many others! Includes 33 demonstration tracks.
00697415 Book/Online Audio $17.99

Hal Leonard Chinese Pipa Method

by Gao Hong

This easy-to-use book serves as an introduction to the Chinese pipa and its techniques. Lessons include: tuning • Western & Chinese notation basics • left and right hand techniques • positions • tremolo • bending • vibrato and overtones • classical pipa repertoire • popular Chinese folk tunes • and more!
00121398 Book/Online Video $19.99

Hal Leonard Dulcimer Method – Second Edition

by Neal Hellman

A beginning method for the Appalachian dulcimer with a unique new approach to solo melody and chord playing. Includes tuning, modes and many beautiful folk songs all demonstrated on the audio accompaniment. Music and tablature.
00699289 Book..$12.99
00697230 Book/Online Audio..........................$19.99

Hal Leonard Flamenco Guitar Method

by Hugh Burns

Traditional Spanish flamenco song forms and classical pieces are used to teach you the basics of the style and technique in this book. Lessons cover: strumming, picking and percussive techniques • arpeggios • improvisation • fingernail tips • capos • and much more. Includes flamenco history and a glossary.
00697363 Book/Online Audio $17.99

Hal Leonard Irish Bouzouki Method

by Roger Landes

This comprehensive method focuses on teaching the basics of the instrument as well as accompaniment techniques for a variety of Irish song forms. It covers: playing position • tuning • picking & strumming patterns • learning the fretboard • accompaniment styles • double jigs, slip jigs & reels • drones • counterpoint • arpeggios • playing with a capo • traditional Irish songs • and more.
00696348 Book/Online Audio $12.99

Hal Leonard Mandolin Method – Second Edition

Noted mandolinist and teacher Rich Del Grosso has authored this excellent mandolin method that features great playable tunes in several styles (bluegrass, country, folk, blues) in standard music notation and tablature. The audio features play-along duets.
00699296 Book..$10.99
00695102 Book/Online Audio..........................$16.99

Hal Leonard Oud Method

by John Bilezikjian

This book teaches the fundamentals of standard Western music notation in the context of oud playing. It also covers: types of ouds, tuning the oud, playing position, how to string the oud, scales, chords, arpeggios, tremolo technique, studies and exercises, songs and rhythms from Armenia and the Middle East, and 25 audio tracks for demonstration and play along.
00695836 Book/Online Audio $14.99

Hal Leonard Sitar Method

by Josh Feinberg

This beginner's guide serves as an introduction to sitar and its technique, as well as the practice, theory, and history of raga music. Lessons include: tuning • postures • right- and left-hand technique • Indian notation • raga forms; melodic patterns • bending strings • hammer-ons, pull-offs, and slides • changing strings • and more!
00696613 Book/Online Audio $16.99
00198245 Book/Online Media $19.99

Hal Leonard Ukulele Method

by Lil' Rev

This comprehensive and easy-to-use beginner's guide by acclaimed performer and uke master Lil' Rev includes many fun songs of different styles to learn and play. Includes: types of ukuleles, tuning, music reading, melody playing, chords, strumming, scales, tremolo, music notation and tablature, a variety of music styles, ukulele history and much more.
00695847 Book 1 Only..$7.99
00695832 Book 1 with Online Audio...............$12.99
00695948 Book 2 Only..$7.99
00695949 Book 2 with Online Audio...............$11.99

HAL•LEONARD®

Visit Hal Leonard Online at
www.halleonard.com

Prices and availability subject to change without notice.

BANJO NOTATION LEGEND

TABLATURE graphically represents the banjo fingerboard. Each horizontal line represents a string, and each number represents a fret.

Strings:
1 D
2 B
3 G
4 D
5 G

4th string, 2nd fret

1st & 2nd strings open, played together

TIME SIGNATURE:
The upper number indicates the number of beats per measure, the lower number indicates that a quarter note gets one beat.

CUT TIME:
Each note's time value should be cut in half. As a result, the music will be played twice as fast as it is written.

QUARTER NOTE:
time value = 1 beat

EIGHTH NOTES:
time value = 1/2 beat each

single   in series

SIXTEENTH NOTES:
time value = 1/4 beat each

single   in series

DOTTED QUARTER NOTE:
time value = 1 1/2 beat

TIE: Pick the 1st note only, then let it sustain for the combined time value.

TRIPLET: Three notes played in the same time normally occupied by two notes of the same time value.

GRACE NOTE: A quickly played note with no time value of its own. The grace note and the note following it only occupy the time value of the second note.

RITARD: A gradual slowing of the tempo or speed of the song.

rit.

QUARTER REST:
time value = 1 beat of silence

EIGHTH REST:
time value = 1/2 beat of silence

HALF REST:
time value = 2 beats of silence

WHOLE REST:
time value = 4 beats of silence

ENDINGS: When a repeated section has a first and second ending, play the first ending only the first time and play the second ending only the second time.

1.   2.

REPEAT SIGNS: Play the music between the repeat signs two times.

D.S. AL CODA:
Play through the music until you complete the measure labeled *"D.S. al Coda,"* then go back to the sign (%).
Then play until you complete the measure labeled *"To Coda ⊕,"* then skip to the section labeled *" ⊕ Coda."*

%   *To Coda* ⊕   *D.S. al Coda*   ⊕ *Coda*

HAMMER-ON: Strike the first (lower) note with one finger, then sound the higher note (on the same string) with another finger by fretting it without picking.

PULL-OFF: Place both fingers on the notes to be sounded. Strike the first note and without picking, pull the finger off to sound the second (lower) note.

SLIDE UP: Strike the first note and then slide the same fret-hand finger up to the second note. The second note is not struck.

SLIDE DOWN: Strike the first note and then slide the same fret-hand finger down to the second note. The second note is not struck.

HALF-STEP CHOKE: Strike the note and bend the string up 1/2 step.

1/2

7

WHOLE-STEP CHOKE: Strike the note and bend the string up one step.

1

10

NATURAL HARMONIC: Strike the note while the fret-hand lightly touches the string directly over the fret indicated.

Harm.

12

BRUSH: Play the notes of the chord indicated by quickly rolling them from bottom to top.

Scruggs/Keith Tuners:

HALF-TWIST UP: Strike the note, twist tuner up 1/2 step, and continue playing.

HALF-TWIST DOWN: Strike the note, twist tuner down 1/2 step, and continue playing.

WHOLE-TWIST UP: Strike the note, twist tuner up one step, and continue playing.

WHOLE-TWIST DOWN: Strike the note, twist tuner down one step, and continue playing.

Right Hand Fingerings

t = thumb   i = index finger   m = middle finger

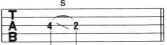